I0529242

UNLOCKING
Your
PURPOSE

KELLIE WILLIAMS

Unlocking Your Purpose
Copyright © 2025 by Kellie Williams
Published by Grace 4 Purpose, Publishing Co. LLC
No parts of this book may be reproduced without written approval
from the author or publisher.
Scripture quotations from The Authorized (King James) Version.
Rights in the Authorized Version in the United Kingdom are
vested in the Crown. Reproduced by permission of the Crown's
patentee, Cambridge University Press
ISBN: 979-8-9926893-4-1
Book cover design by Grace 4 Purpose Publishing Co. LLC
Printed and bound in the United States of America

Unlocking Your Purpose

Kellie Williams

Table of Contents

Introduction

I started writing this book when I was just nineteen years old because I believe God called me to share a testimony that is bigger than me, for a greater purpose. I am a saved, sanctified, Holy Ghost filled believer who loves God with everything in me. I'm not ashamed of the gospel. I am not ashamed to praise God, or to speak of His goodness. I chose this life. I wasn't pressured to get saved, I made the decision on my own to live holy, and I stand by it every day.

I know that being saved is not enough to keep me every day. It's my daily prayer that God fills me with His Holy Spirit and until He does, I will continue seeking Him with everything I have.

I am a proud member of New Generation Church, where I have been attending for about eight years. Under the leadership of Supt. Eric Andrews and First Lady Sheree Andrews, I have grown immensely. Their guidance has played a significant role in me finding my purpose in life.

Through this ministry, I've not only developed a real relationship with God, but I've also learned how to read and understand His Word, how to praise and worship freely, and how to recognize the presence of God in my everyday life. I've let go of past hurts, and released the wrongful words spoken over my life. Was it easy? No. But it was necessary. When you trust God, you trust that He knows what's best through it all; even when you don't understand.

When I gave my life to Christ, got filled with the Holy Ghost, and fully stepped into my walk as a believer, so many questions flooded my mind: *What's next? What did God create me to do? Surely, it's more than just spreading the gospel... right?* I remember crying out to God, "What is my purpose?" I often heard people say, *there's a reason you're still here,* and though I didn't fully grasp it then, those words stuck with me. I kept searching for that reason, wondering how my purpose would not only change my life but also impact the lives of others.

As you read this book and journey through my experiences, it's my deepest prayer that it draws you closer to God and helps you unlock your own purpose. Maybe you've felt lost before, like you were just going through the motions. I know that feeling all too well. I've been there before, making progress, only to feel like I was set back twenty steps. But one thing I've come to know is this: your purpose will push you into a place in God that you never imagined you could go.

UNLOCKING YOUR PURPOSE

This book is more than my story, it's an invitation for you to unlock your own purpose.

UNLOCKING YOUR PURPOSE

Chapter One

What does it mean to have purpose in God?

When I think of the word purpose it makes me think of it as a divine or intentional reasons for something being done. I am reminded of Jeremiah 29:11, which states, *"For I know the plans I have for you declares the Lord plans to prosper you, and not to harm you, plans to give you hope and a future"*. This scripture is a reminder that God's plans and purpose for our lives is to help us to reach success but we will have to endure some things that will help build our character, develop us, grow in our faith and to prepare us. In my mindset at the time, I thought I was pursuing the purpose God had for me by being saved, filled with the Holy Ghost, going to church and doing everything else that was required of me as a believer. The more time I spent with God, He began to show me what it really means to have purpose in Him. When it comes to our purpose, we must understand that everyone will have a different purpose in life but it will still glorify Him. In 1 Corinthians 10:31 it says, *"whether therefore ye eat, or drink, or whatsoever ye do, do it all to the glory of God."* Be intentional about everything you're doing to glorify God. Take a moment and ask yourself, *Am I doing these things to please my flesh or to please my heavenly Father?*

During my transitions from middle school to high school, I faced challenges that left me feeling alone and confused. I did not have a mentor to guide me at first; I was just going through so much and I could not really talk to my parents. There were so many moments I wanted to give up, and just throw in the towel. I was suffering from depression, anxiety, constant worry, stress, low self-esteem, and suicidal thoughts. It was just so much for me to handle at the time. I did not know what was happening to me. Although I believed in God, I was saved and had developed a relationship with Him, I still felt clueless to what my purpose was. Why would God allow me to go through this? I never thought this little old Kellie would be worth something, or have value, but God truly revealed some things to me. I never thought God would start to use me at a young age which is so amazing. I just stand in awe of God every day.

As I began to grow and mature, I started to really develop a relationship with God. I remember going to church with my granny and auntie under temporary watch care until one day my mom found a church that she wanted us to come visit with her. At the time, it was hard to leave something I was so comfortable with to step into the unknown. I put my fear of change to the side because I believed this transition was going to push me into the right direction. God was preparing me for a purpose that was bigger than me. I knew I needed to trust His direction. I did not realize how much joining New Generation Church was about to transform my whole life. Although I knew joining this church was going to change my life I still had questions about the things I was having to endure, my purpose and my walk in Christ.

Have you ever had moments where you wonder, *why did this have to happen to me? What am I doing wrong that would cause this? Why do I have to go through this and not others?* I remember having moments like where I would have all these questions about why this was happening. It wasn't until my sophomore year in high school to realize that it was nothing that I did that caused this to happen. It was just the way life was and after going through so much in life I begin to realize God has purpose on my life and that when you have purpose on your life you will go through something. Romans 5:3-5 is a reminder of how God allows us to go through trials and tribulations to build our character, faith and to even develop us in Him. Joining New Generation Church really changed my life. I was delivered from depression, suicide, low self-esteem, and peer pressure. I learned what the true foundation of holiness means, learned how to pray, how to worship and praise God, and I even learned how to connect with

God on a different level. This ministry has taught me so much and I'm proud to be a member. I never experienced the presence of God until joining ministry. There is so much encouragement and words of wisdom that I received.. It was through this ministry that God began to show me my purpose.

One of the things I learned is the more you continue to seek the face of God, no matter what you may be facing, God will begin to show you the purpose behind your storm, your tears, and your frustration. He will even show you that the attacks that came wasn't about you.

It was hard for me to understand the purpose that God had for me because I was so consumed by things that happened to me and I couldn't understand why the Lord would allow me to encounter it. From middle school through high school; I had experienced so much and I just didn't think I would be able to move forward. I thought I was just going to be stuck in this box forever but that changed when I came to this ministry. It was not until I graduated from high school when I truly felt free.

There will be moments in life that will try to tear you down and make you want to give up on life. I am sharing my own experiences to encourage you to continuing pushing through the suffering; no matter what. Even as I face different challenges throughout my life's journey today I'm learning that it's not about what the outcome will be and why I'm having to deal with this. It's mainly about how you handle the challenges of life and how you survived it. I can remember when I dealt with all sorts of things; death in the family, failing tests, low self-esteem, getting involved with the wrong crowd and so much more. I would question myself, "God why did I have to go through this? Why did you allow these things to happen in my life?"

Throughout my life, I learned to never question God; even when going through tough situations. No matter how bad things may get, you will overcome it; just trust that the God we serve will bring you out. It will not always be perfect but I encourage you to trust God because through the good, the bad, the ups and downs, God will see you through. Don't be so quick to throw in the towel because that's where the enemy comes in and tries to trick you.

I am a living witness that when you keep pressing forward no matter how you feel, no matter how uncertain the path is, things will get better, especially when you keep God at the center of your life. Have you ever paused to consider that maybe the trial you are facing isn't meant to break you, but to build you. I've had to stop and ask myself: what if the storms I am facing right now could actually be preparing me for where God is leading me, and showing me what I couldn't see before? Be intentional in the storm you are facing. I want to encourage you to be intentional about the storm you are facing. It may feel difficult, but don't just survive it, learn from it. Grow through it and remember that there is a greater purpose coming out of it.

Dear God,

Thank you for this time of sharing and recognizing what it means to have purpose in you. Lord, I pray that your will be done in every area of our lives so that you may get all of the glory. Lord, I pray that you would help us to look past our flesh when we are facing trials and tribulations. Help us to see that they are working for our good in the long run. Lord, help us to stay focused in the midst of the storms we face by fasting, consecrating, and reading our Word. Help us to understand that the trials we face are here to build our faith in you and not our flesh. Teach us to rely on you more, trust you more, and to seek you first more than other things. I pray that even as we reflect in our own time, may we gain more spiritual insight through the Word of God. May we rely on Ecclesiastes 3:1, which is a reminder of God's different purposes for different seasons of our lives but it's all going to work out for our good? Lord, help us to put on our spiritual glasses so we don't assume every storm is to hinder or hurt us.

I pray you would help us to examine ourselves as we strive to find our purpose in you. I pray that as we have our moments of doubts, fear, frustration and even sadness that you will not allow us to stay there. Colossians 1:13-14 reminds us, *for in him all things were created: things in heaven and on earth, visible and invisible, whether thrones or powers or rulers or authorities; all things have been created through him and for him.* It's a reminder that God allows trials and tribulations to test our faith in Him and to see if we are still standing for Him. My prayer is that God would continue to mold us into the person He is calling us to be and not fold every time a storm comes to shake our faith.

In Jesus' Name,
Amen

Reflection Questions:

1. Why is purpose so important in my walk with Christ?
2. How do I keep pushing when I want to quit?
3. Why is my faith being tested?
4. What is my purpose?

UNLOCKING YOUR PURPOSE

Chapter Two:
My Journey as a Young Believer

When I first started attending New Generation Church, I was saved but my walk with God felt shallow. It was there that I rededicated my life to Christ, not because I had turned away from Him, but because I wanted to ensure my life was fully aligned with His will. As a young believer I questioned why the Lord was calling me so young. I believe God was calling me to be an example and to share of His faithfulness that you can still live holy and enjoy life. At first I was uncertain. Would people even take me seriously?

I was reminded of 1 Timothy 4:12: *"Let no man despise thy youth but be thou an example of the believers, in word, in conversation, in charity, in spirit, in faith, in purity"*. It's a reminder that being young does not count you out. You can still draw people back to God, even at a young age.

Throughout middle school, high school and college, I faced challenges while navigating environments where people wanted to love God but they also wanted to embrace worldly behaviors. I knew when I rededicated my life to Christ that it was not going to be easy, but I was committed to staying in the path that God had placed me on.

Have you ever felt scared to step out and do something? Felt alone, or felt like no one would understand where you are in life? That was how I felt most of the time throughout school because it felt like every person I would try to connect with would try to tempt me into compromising my walk. I had to learn that not everyone could be in my circle. Romans 12:2 reminds us, *"And be not conformed to this world: but be ye transformed by the renewing of your mind, that ye may prove what is that good, and acceptable, and perfect, will of God."* As young believers we do not have to accept or participate in the patterns of what the world is doing. We have been called to make a difference, and to keep the standard of holiness.

Right now, I'm in a season in my life where I'm learning to be grateful for where I am, even if I'm not where I really want to be. The most important part of my walk with Christ is to cherish every moment or encounter with God. These moments remind me that God brought me out of some things and some places, and for that, I rejoice. Sometimes there are no words to describe what I feel during those close encounters with God. I remember a time when I was praying at our old church, crying out at the altar for the Holy Ghost. I kept seeking and asking, but after a while, I began to feel discouraged. Someone reminded me not to give up on seeking the Holy Ghost.

Then came Pentecost Sunday. We all came to the altar, and I felt something move in my Spirit. After I went back to my seat, I still felt that release. When Pastor laid hands on me, I began speaking in my Holy Ghost language. People surrounded me as I worshipped; it took a while for me to actually calm down. That Pentecost Sunday will always be one to remember, because I wasn't just refilled, I was set free.

It reminded me: never doubt what God has given you. He doesn't take it back. It's yours. God reminded me not to doubt the power within me, not just when I speak, but when I pray. Proverbs 18:21 says, *"Death and life are in the power of the tongue."* That's a reminder to use the power God has given us.

Sometimes we have so much doubt about what we believe or what we prayed for. James 1:6-8 reminds us, *"But let him ask in faith, nothing wavering. For he that wavereth is like a wave of the sea driven with the wind and tossed. For let not man think that he shall receive anything of the Lord. A double minded man is unstable in all his ways."* If we believe God to do the impossible than we cannot be doubtful too. When we come to God in Prayer, we have to believe God will fulfill what we are asking for according to His will. We think what we prayed for is supposed to happen when we want it to happen but that's not how it works; it happens on God's timing not ours.

Have you ever had a moment where you became doubtful because it didn't happen in your timing? Lord when is it going to happen for me? Why has it not happen yet? Are you even listening to me? In Proverbs 3:5-6 reminds us to " Trust in the Lord with all thine heart; and lean not unto thine own understanding. In all thy ways acknowledge him, and he shall direct thy paths". It's a reminder to trust God's timing for whatever you are believing Him to do. Anytime doubt comes to my mind, I speak the Word of God over my situation. Whatever you may be believing God for, just trust the timing even when it may seem like God is not answering you.

Have you ever felt tired of taking tests every year in school just to prove you can move to the next grade? Spiritually, it is the same. In order to grow into the person God called you to be, you'll go through tests, trials, and tribulations that will stretch your faith. John 16:33 it says, *"These things I have spoken unto you, that in me ye might have peace. In the world ye shall have tribulation: but be of good cheer; I have overcome the world. "* The trials are not to destroy you—they're to birth something greater within you.

Declare the Word over your life: you are worth it, you are anointed, and *you can* do whatever the Lord called you to do. Sometimes we think, *I can't take much more of this,* but when you truly realize what God is getting ready to manifest through you, you find the strength to press forward. Galatians 6:9 says, *"And let us not be weary in well doing: for in due season we shall reap, if we faint not."* Don't quit. Keep pressing

I know what it's like to feel alone, depressed, battle with low self-esteem, have a lack of confidence in your anointing, deal with depression, and feel as if you are no longer needed on this Earth. Attending New Generation Church has caused a mindset shift in me, I no longer battle with those negative thoughts. I realized that the enemy wanted me to continue having these thoughts that were not of God... My pastor said something that has stuck with me, "If you are alive in this world, then God has a purpose for you

To the person reading this: you are never alone. God is always with you. Joshua 1:9 it says, *"Have not I commanded thee? Be strong and of a good courage; be not afraid, neither be thou dismayed: for the Lord thy God is with thee whithersoever thou goest."* Sometimes as young people, it is hard for us to open up, especially when we feel misunderstood. I've been there before. There were times when people spoke so negatively about me that I wanted to give up, but I had to learn that God loves me, and He is always there for me, no matter what happens.

Have you ever questioned God's love for you? Maybe even questioned how smart or talented you are? At one point in my life I didn't even think I had a purpose. And I didn't think I could be anointed. But I've come to realize that even when we can't see what God is doing, He's preparing something greater.

We never know whose watching or what people might say, but it doesn't matter. What matters is staying true to who God created you to be. I recently watched an old video of myself giving a mini message before I left for college. I titled it 'It's Not Easy, But It's Necessary.' That message still encourages me today. As I end my freshman year and prepared to return for that sophomore year, I understand now more than ever: the trials may not be easy, but they're necessary for where God is taking me.

No matter who you are in life, young or old, God has a purpose for your life. You are never alone. You can achieve every dream and passion with God's help. Matthew 6:33 reminds us, *"But seek ye first the kingdom of God, and His righteousness; and all these things shall be added unto you."* When you seek God for real, with no agenda, He hears you. There are no words to describe what I feel every time I come into His presence.

Dear God,

Thank You for the journey You've placed me on, because it has brought me to where I am today. I understand now that these trials are not here to break me, but to build me for the place You are calling me to. I pray that You continue to guide me through this journey.

Your Word says in **Psalm 119:105,** *"Thy word is a lamp unto my feet, and a light unto my path."* Lord, in this world full of uncertainty, remind us that our help comes from You. Lead us through the unknown. Help us to draw closer to You and go deeper in Your Word.

We trust the path You have set before us. Give us the courage to endure the battles we may face along the way. Strengthen us not to lean on our own understanding, but to trust fully in Your will for our lives. Teach us to grow through our trials and to depend on You in everything.

Lord, cover our minds in the midst of every test and trial. Your Word says in Philippians 2:5, "Let this mind be in you, which was also in Christ Jesus." Help us to stay focused when distractions come and try to pull us away from You.

**In Jesus' Name,
Amen.**

Reflection questions:
1. Am I spending enough time with God?
2. What is the purpose of this trial?
3. Why is God allowing me to go through this storm?
4. Am I spending more time with my flesh?

UNLOCKING YOUR PURPOSE

Chapter Three:
The Journey of Being a Young Believer in School

Have you ever been so excited to start something new, only to get disappointed because it wasn't what you were expecting? That's exactly how I felt at several points throughout my school years. My faith was tested like never before, from being in the wrong crowds, failing tests, hearing negative words, losing loved ones, being picked on, and so much more. But In the midst of every challenge, God helped me overcome.

When it came to being a young believer in school I knew it wasn't going to be easy but I knew that God was going to be with me. Romans 8:28 is a reminder that, *"God makes all things work together for our good.."* Looking back, I see now that even the most painful moments were working together for my good.

In middle school, I failed my STAAR tests in both math and reading. I was depressed and I did not know what to do next. When I first got the news that I didn't pass I felt like a complete failure. I watched how other kids would go do other activities, but I had to stay back in the classroom to relearn the material. I beat myself up so badly, calling myself stupid, dumb, and feeling completely unmotivated and discouraged.

Have you ever felt so disappointed that you started questioning everything? I remember asking myself was it really worth it? That season of my life was really dark. At that time I couldn't see a way out. I thank God for my praying First Lady who never gave up on me. I remember being in such a low place that I didn't really want to talk to anyone because talking about it made me actually cry about it even more. I remember a conversation I had with My First Lady, and she really encouraged me, and prayed me through which help me shift my perspective... If you don't pass the first time, it's okay. She helped me to see that maybe God is making a testimony to share with others.

High school brought new challenges. I was so excited to start my journey as a freshman, but that quickly changed when I got there. There were so many cliques, so many expectations, and so much pressure.

Through my whole four years of high school I gave people the power of control by allowing them to walk all over me and it was like every year something bad was happening to me, but that changed as soon as I began to be fully dedicated and committed to my relationship with God

I ended up hanging around the wrong crowd. I thought I had the right friends, but one altercation flipped everything. I was talked about, cursed out, and picked on. I knew in that moment I was under a spiritual attack because of the calling on my life.

I remember getting ready to finish up my last year in High School and the challenges still had not stopped. It felt like I couldn't catch a break. I remember receiving the news of my granny from my dad's side passing away. It was hard for me to stay focused, but I kept pushing... I had to stay in the Word of God and remind myself that all these things are still going to work for my good. Romans 8:18 says, *"For I reckon that the sufferings of this present time are not worthy to be compared with the glory which shall be revealed in us. "That scripture brought me comfort and reminded me* that I would see her again. It helped me refocus.

While grieving this loss, I was still facing challenges in school. I was dealing with a teacher in one of my classes who treated me as if I was a joke. I cried about it so many times. But it was through prayer that I found the strength to keep showing up to that class until the semester ended. I remember saying, "God if I can just make it to the finish line and walk across that stage." And I did. Walking across that stage on graduation day was so exciting. My soul was rejoicing knowing I didn't have to look back.

Starting my college journey at Texas A&M University Commerce was exciting. I was ready to explore and experience new and wonderful things. I was so excited about what God had in store for me. I was confident that He would guide me through this journey. College, like everything else, had its own set of challenges. After my freshman year, I realized I needed to pray more, and be watchful about who I connected myself to.

1 Peter 5:8 it says, *"Be sober, be vigilant; because your adversary the devil, as a roaring lion, walketh about, seeking whom he may devour."* It was through this scripture that I began to realign my focus in college. I got so caught up in wanting to fit in and have friends that I was willing to compromise who I was. After my freshmen year, I learned to just be who God made me to be and just stay true to myself and stop trying to please others. In the scripture Jeremiah 1:5 reminds us *"Before I formed thee in the belly I knew thee: and before thou camest forth out of the womb I sanctify thee, and I ordained thee a prophet unto the nations".* This is a reminder that God already knew we were born to be made set apart from the patterns of this world. It was through this moment I had to spend more time in the word of God and in prayer each school year.

I remember being invited by a roommate to go to a party, a part of me wanted to go, thinking I could make more friends. But something in me said, "Don't go I ended up staying behind, and I am so glad I did. I knew that if I would have went it would have been going in the opposite direction. That moment reminded me to ask myself: *Is it really worth it to follow the crowd?*

During my sophomore year, I started to pray and ask God to connect me with more like-minded believers around campus.
That prayer was answered the day I met my roommate, Lauren. Overtime, we got to know each other and she told me she wanted to start doing a Bible study group. I told her I would love to join a Bible study group because I was looking for an accountable person where we could stay connected in the Word of God.

Romans 15: 5 it says, *"Now the God of patience and consolation grant you to be likeminded one toward another according to Christ Jesus.* "That Bible study group blessed me, and reminded me that's it's important to be connected to likeminded believers. Ask yourself, *are you surrounded by people who push you closer to God?*

One of the highlights of my college journey was junior year. I had professors who pushed me out of my comfort zone with writing, which stretched me creatively. I started thinking outside the box and believing more in my voice. I held onto 1 John 4:4: *"Greater is he that is in you, than he that is in the world."* That scripture reminded me that I could overcome anything with God by my side.

By the time I reached my junior and senior years, I had moments where I felt like enough was enough. The only thing keeping me motivated was knowing it would all be worth it in the end.

Joshua 1:9 became my anchor: *"Have not I commanded thee? Be strong and of a good courage; be not afraid, neither be thou dismayed: for the Lord thy God is with thee whithersoever thou goest."* That verse reminded me I wasn't alone.

But then I faced another huge challenge: losing major loved ones. That was one of the most difficult moments of my life. It tested my faith deeply, but it also brought me closer to God than ever before. I struggled with my assignments, didn't want to leave my dorm, and questioned why it all had to happen, even after I prayed. Have you ever asked, "Why, God? Why now?" Even with support from church and friends, I knew I needed time alone with God. I turned my dorm room into an altar. I cried out to Him, and it was in that moment He reminded me: There is more purpose in you that you haven't even unlocked yet. That moment shifted my entire relationship with Him. Knowing God for myself has changed how I handle life.

This was a major milestone in my life because it has shown me how God has purpose on my life and at the time I didn't know what that purpose was going to be. I had to stay focus and I could not connect with everyone. It was through this moment of being in with the wrong crowd that has helped me to see that everyone does not always have the best intentions for me. I had to increase my prayer time and seek God in areas where I was struggling to walk alone in.

I learned to rely on God for myself and not based on other people relationships. If I can be transparent with you, sometimes that can be difficult because of the weight of your problems, challenges and even storms you are facing. When you make that sacrifice with God, He will bless you tremendously but we must be willing to put in the effort. I want to encourage you to set aside time in to spend time with God because it can go a long way for you. Sometimes it can be difficult finding time with God but even if its ten minutes a day that is a start to build your walk with God.

As I reflect on these pivotal moments that have shifted my walk with God, I now see God was transforming my life the entire time. Failing those tests? They gave me a new perspective. Instead of complaining, I started asking the Lord, "What are you preparing me for? Help me to have patience as I am going through this time."

Take a moment to reflect. Whatever you are going through, it is just a season, It's not forever. James 1:2-4 reminds us,, *"My Brethren, count it all joy when ye fall into divers temptations; Knowing this, that the trying of your faith worketh patience. But let patience have her perfect work, that ye may be perfect and entire, wanting nothing."*

Trials don't come to break you, but to build your faith/. There were times when I was facing those trials that I wanted to throw in the towel and commit suicide. The Lord would not let me stay there. Sometimes, it takes a prayer, a conversation, or a moment of stillness to see things differently. For me, it was reaching out to my First Lady and hearing, "God's not done with you yet." It was the Lord connecting me with a likeminded roommate and a Bible study group. I may not have always gotten the answers I hoped for, but I've come out stronger, and my story is still being written.

Dear God,

Today, I thank You for being with us through every challenge, every storm, and every situation we may face. I pray that You continue to teach us to rely on You, on the good days, the hard days, in our low moments, and when all seems well.

Lord, we trust in Your plan, Your process, and Your perfect will for our lives. We thank You even for the rejections and the losses, because we believe they are part of the greater good You are working out for us.

We ask for Your divine wisdom, knowledge, and guidance through Your Word as we walk this journey of faith. Help us to hold tight to the promise of Isaiah 43:2:
"When thou passest through the waters, I will be with thee; and through the rivers, they shall not overflow thee: when thou walkest through the fire, thou shalt not be burned; neither shall the flame kindle upon thee."
May this be a reminder that no matter what we face, you are with us. You will not fail us, you will see us through.

Lord, teach us to depend on Your Word more than the opinions and expectations of society. Help us to be true ambassadors for Christ, not conforming to the ways of this world. As Your Word says in Romans 12:2:
"And be not conformed to this world: but be ye transformed by the renewing of your mind, that ye may prove what is that good, and acceptable, and perfect, will of God."

UNLOCKING YOUR PURPOSE

Help us, Lord, to speak life over our lives. Let us believe that every time we speak Your truth and Your promises, they will manifest according to Your will.

In Jesus' Name,
Amen

Reflection Questions

1. What purpose are you trying to show me through this trial?
2. Am I being my own hindrance by rushing the process God is taking me though?
3. Is God really listening?
4. How will this help me down the path you are taking me on?

Chapter Four:
Identifying your Purpose

It was through New Generation Church where I truly
began to find myself, spiritually and naturally. As I
continued attending this ministry, I remember being
new and just learning who the leaders were and getting
familiar with everything; I had a humble and sweet
spirit, and I wanted to be a blessing to my leaders, but
financially I couldn't do much because I was still
searching for a job.

It was hard because God knew my heart and desires. I
started to think about writing a letter but I was not sure
if it would be enough. It felt small at the time.
However, I went ahead and gave my pastor a birthday
letter; I was nervous and hesitant, what if he didn't like
it? But when he told me he loved it, it stirred something
in me. I had always written in journals, but I had never
written actual letters like that before.

After that experience, I felt led by God to start writing
encouraging letters to both my pastor and first lady. I
never imagined that eleven years later, I'd still be
writing. I share this memory because it remains close to
my heart. It reminds me that God truly sees the desires
of our hearts. Even when we don't have money or
resources, He uses what we do have.

I shared this moment because it helped me to discover my passion for writing. A gift God placed within me. It showed me that purpose is not always tied to material things, but to the talents and callings God gives us to use for His glory. I'm reminded of 1 Peter 4:10-11 which says, *"As every man hath received the gift, even so minister the same one to another, as good stewards of the manifold grace of God. If any man speak, let him speak as the oracles of God; if any man minister, let him do it as of the ability which God giveth: that God in all things may be glorified through Jesus Christ, to whom be praise and dominion for ever and ever. Amen."* I am so humbled to use my gift to write encouraging letters, and I truly thank God for placing the desire in my heart and starting me on this journey of writing.

Have you ever known deep down that you wanted to make a difference, but you didn't know where or how to begin? I remember asking the Lord, *"Is this really what you desire for me to do? What if they don't even read it? What if the letters just get tossed aside?"* I had all of these doubtful thoughts in my mind when I started writing encouraging letters.

When it comes to identifying our purpose, it's important to pray for God's will to be revealed. I prayed several times, even after completing the letters, because I wanted to be sure that this is what the Lord wanted me to do. I had no idea how God would use writing to lead me into my purpose.

I approached each encouraging letter as if it were a paper I was writing for school. I would meditate on specific scriptures that the Lord would speak to me concerning their letters. I've enjoyed writing since Middle school, especially when we had free writing topics, because I could truly express myself. I believe God used my classroom experiences to sharpen my writing gift, even before I fully understood its purpose. Now, when I write, I don't see it as a task, but I see it as an assignment from God. Each letter is an opportunity to encourage, uplift, and point someone back to Him. Sometimes the Lord would give me wisdom to write *before* I even start writing the letters. As I wrote, I could almost visualize the message ministering to the person of what God's Word said about them.

The first step in identifying my purpose was prayer. It wasn't just one prayer, it was a process. In Philippians 4:6-7 it says, *"Be careful for nothing; but in everything by prayer and supplication with thanksgiving let your requests be made known unto God. And the peace of God, which passeth all understanding, shall keep your hearts and minds through Christ Jesus."* We must pray about everything so that God's will can be done. I knew that even after I got saved and filled with the Holy

Ghost, that there was more work the Lord had to do within me before He revealed my purpose.

 It wasn't until I got closer to my senior year in college that God began to reveal more to me concerning my purpose with writing. He showed me that my writing was more than a hobby, it was a ministry. From starting a YouTube channel to spreading the gospel of Jesus Christ, I knew there was more work ahead of me.

As my passion for writing grew, I began to see that this gift extended far beyond letters. This became especially clear during my college years, through classes like American Literature, British Literature, and Literature and Film. These courses pushed me in ways I never expected. The topics challenged me to think critically and creatively, often imagining myself living in different time periods.
My Literature and Film class was especially challenging because we had to write essays based on the films we watched or books we read. I enjoyed writing in my English courses because they pushed me to think outside the box, especially when writing argumentative papers. My American Literature and Advanced Creative Writing classes helped shape my purpose by teaching me to go deeper than just the words on a page. My focus shifted from just turning in an assignment to making an impact on someone's life.

One of my biggest challenges was feeling like my age disqualified me. But 1 Timothy 4:12 reminded me, *"Let no man despise thy youth; but be thou an example of the believers..."* That verse pushed me to continue being the example God called me to be.

Throughout my college journey, I had moments of deep worship, fasting, weeping, and travailing. I asked God why I had to endure certain things, but those low places reminded me that there is still more inside of me. Even pain has purpose, and God can use our hardest moments to help us identify His call on our lives.

Have you ever received a mandate from God but felt unsure about it? I did. I had so many questions: *"Lord, are You sure? Is this really what You want me to do?"* I knew my purpose would grow beyond just writing, but I didn't expect it to begin through an online YouTube channel.

When the Lord placed it in my spirit, I hesitated. I didn't want to do it just because everyone else was doing it during the pandemic. I prayed and prayed because I wanted confirmation that this was really God's will for me.

Proverbs 10:17 reminds us: *"He is in the way of life that keepeth instruction: but he that refuseth reproof erreth."*

UNLOCKING YOUR PURPOSE

I launched my YouTube channel in my sophomore year of college, right in the middle of the pandemic. God sent confirmation through the multiple people who were watching. Even after experiencing personal loss, I was reminded in a dream that God was calling me back to purpose. Yes, it's okay to grieve, but don't neglect your time with Him.

A wise person once told me: *"Prayer will carry you through the hardest trials and tribulations."* As I continue to walk in what God has called me to do, my heart's desire is to stay humble and surrendered.

Your purpose won't always be revealed overnight. Often, it's a journey that unfolds through experiences, struggles, and obedience. We all face challenges, but we must stay focused. The enemy wants to distract us from purpose, but if we stay rooted in prayer, fasting, and God's Word, we can remain aligned.

1 Thessalonians 5:16-18 reminds us: "Rejoice evermore. Pray without ceasing. In everything give thanks…"

That's a reminder to always rejoice, pray, and stay grateful. So ask yourself:

"Do my desires align with God's will for my life?"

UNLOCKING YOUR PURPOSE

We are always learning and evolving as believers. I've come to understand that in every struggle, storm, and hidden pain, God is writing a greater story. We may not always understand it, but greater is coming. Even when it's hard, your obedience matters because someone is depending on your encouragement.

When you identify your purpose, remember:

Keep praying.

Stay focused, even in trials.

Recognize that your purpose is bigger than you, it's for the Glory of God.

UNLOCKING YOUR PURPOSE

Dear God,

Thank You for helping us to identify our purpose in You. Thank You for new strength, divine guidance, joy, and wisdom to keep pressing forward, even in the midst of every storm.

Forgive us, Lord, for the times we've complained about the very things You've allowed to shape and strengthen us. Help us to trust You through every struggle, every pain, every battle, and every moment of hurt. Help us to recognize that there is purpose even in the battles, the wars, and the strongholds we face.

Lord, we ask that Your will be done in our lives. We surrender fully to Your plan, Your purpose, and Your divine will. We decree and declare victory over our lives, and we commit to walking boldly into everything You've ordained for us.

Teach us to stay in prayer long enough to hear Your voice, especially when we pour out our hearts and desires to You. Strengthen us to remain faithful even when we don't receive the answer right away. Guard our hearts from giving up or conforming to the patterns of this world.

We pray for renewed boldness, fresh confidence, and unwavering trust in You.

**In Jesus' Name,
Amen.**

Reflection questions

1. Is this God's will or my own will?
2. Am I praying long enough to hear God's Voice?
3. Am I giving into the enemy plot by quitting?
4. Why does purpose cause so much pain?

UNLOCKING YOUR PURPOSE

Chapter Five:
Questioning My Purpose

I remember after my freshmen year of high school I was ready to quit because it was so much and I didn't understand why I had to experience this. I had so many questions of why me? What did I do wrong? Why is this happening? I was frustrated, embarrassed, sad, tired of pretending, depressed and overwhelmed and so many more emotions I was feeling. It was a lot for me to a point it was hard for me to focus on how to keep going because it felt like weights, I could not get rid of. Even as a young believer I had so many thoughts of lord why I am going through this so young? I was questioning my purpose through middle and high school? I remember receiving bad news concerning my STAAR tests it felt so embarrassing and I kept speaking negativity over myself and questioning my abilities. So many moments when I was question myself and abilities if I'm good enough or smart enough to do this?

Every now and then you must take a deep breath to remind yourself that this is only a phase that is building you for where God is taking you. I believe we live in a society where we have all the standards and expectations of the way people should look, dress, what type of phone they should carry, the latest shoes that came out and etc. I believe we should break that cycle of expectations that most time can happen in schools and sometimes in churches. One of the biggest things I struggled with in middle school and high school is the expectations people set, failing tests, wrongful words spoken, wrong crowd. All of these things had me questioning my purpose and although there were moments where I knew this was for a greater purpose at the time I couldn't see it.

When it comes to these expectations in society, school, and church sometimes people aren't aware of how it can impact a person in many ways. For myself in middle school and high school I struggled with feeling the need of people opinions, needing to meet these expectations so I can fit in, insecure about myself. These moments had me questioning my purpose and causing me to feel like I could not achieve it. Although I knew God was developing my purpose from the start of middle school, I still could not see it yet because I was still in my own world. I am reminded of James 4:6, *"But he giveth more grace. Wherefore he saith, God resisteth the proud, but giveth grace unto the humble."*

All my life I have known God for myself but my faith has been tested even the more since I started middle school, high school and even college. I have never been one to question God even when going through things because in my mindset I know it's for a greater purpose. When I failed my tests in school it made me question God like never before. I believe God will answer prayers if it's according to his will. In my mind I just believe that God's will was for me to pass the test the first time. When it didn't happen like that it made me question myself, who God is, the love God has for me, my purpose in life. I believe we all have moments where we question God for allowing us to go through this storm or season, we may be in. We cannot stay there because the more we go through the more God continues to show us His will for our lives. In Isaiah 55:8-9 it says, *"For my thoughts are not your thoughts, neither are your ways my ways, saith the Lord. For as the heavens are higher than the earth, so are my ways higher than your ways, and my thoughts than your thought."* I'm reminded that it's important to always pray for God's will to be done in every aspect of our lives. It's important that we allow God to connect us to people who are on different levels than us.

I believe connecting with my first lady during my lowest moment when I failed major tests was needed because I couldn't understand certain things through my own eyes but someone who's been through enough to know why we go through difficult storms. When it came to transitioning to a new church I believe God knew something bigger was happening within myself as I prayed more. I will always remember my family church, Deliverance Tabernacle because that's where my true foundation started of praying, seeking God for myself, started reading my bible. When transitioning to a new church it was a little emotional for myself but I knew God was taking me to a greater place in Him. When I came to New Generation church, I felt like a baby in Christ all over because I knew God was doing a work in me all over again. Although I knew how to pray, read my Word, etc., I knew God was requiring more out of me. I learned how to really connect with God daily outside of Sunday and mid-week worship. One of the biggest things I learned was the importance of building a relationship with God every day and not waiting until Sunday to start building an altar. The biggest Impact was being save and filled with the Holy Ghost because that is when God begin to take me deeper through the Word of God and in intercession time with him. I learned how to really worship and praise God for myself. Therefore, knowing how to really seek the Lord for myself, learning how to really worship and praise, understanding the importance of the word of God has helped prepared me for my transition to college and even identifying my purpose. Although these moments tested my faith and had me questioning my purpose I knew God was still working on me. I could see the purpose God had for me but was blindsided because of the challenges I was facing.

UNLOCKING YOUR PURPOSE

When I came to college I knew that there will be times where my faith will be tried by temptation, worldly patterns and other worldly desires that may be out there in society. I remember when my campus had a tragedy and there were times I wanted to call my leaders but the Lord allow me to turn my dorm room into an alter and lay out before Him in prayer.

It was through much prayer, fasting, consecrate in God that I begin to understand things a little bit more concerning His will, the purpose he has for my life, the importance of spending the quality time with him daily and spending time in the word of God. I will forever be grateful for the shift God allowed to happen when it came to transitioning to a new church because my life has truly change. I have learned how to spend a little bit more time in prayer and don't be so quick to get up after five minutes even when it comes to praising and worshiping God. I learned so much in my walk with God at a young age because of the leadership I am under. I have been able to identify my purpose, develop a stronger relationship with God, grow my faith and more. I have learned to turn my face to the wall instead of questioning everything the Lord was allowing me to go through.

I learned from my personal experiences that I can't just depend on my parents, pastor or, first lady's prayers; I had to develop my own true relationship with God. I have found myself in my dorm room crying out aloud to God in prayer not worrying about if my roommate has an issue with it. When you truly have a deep relationship with God you will not worry about what others would say or think, you will just be in the moment with God. I've transformed my dorm room into an altar of worship. It's not about seeking God for blessings but simply longing to hear His voice. The moments, when I pour out my heart in prayer have become the most sacred and transformative times in my life. These moments is how I have been able to fight the questions, doubts and insecurities concerning my purpose.

I know most of you will probably feel scared, insecure, or even not ready but that is what the purpose of me becoming a Christian author to not only just write a biography but to write a book that will help inspire you to come out of your comfort zone in certain things. I was that person that was scared to pray because I was afraid that people would think I was talking to myself. I was that person who was scared to go to the alter because I was afraid people would judge me for being young and pretending like I was not going through anything. I was that person who was insecure because I was afraid that God could not use me at a young age. I want to challenge you by asking this? Am I hindering my own self from pursuing the purpose God has for me? Take a moment and think is this God's will for me to be scared, insecure, and doubtful? In Ephesians 4:29

its says, *"Let no corrupt communication proceed out of your mouth, but that which is good to the use of edifying, that it may minister grace unto the hearers"*. This is your reminder to speak the word of God over your life no matter what you or someone else may face. It's important to speak victory over your life and encourage someone else to declare it as well.

Dear God,

Today, I thank You for giving me the power to speak life over myself and everyone connected to me. Thank You for placing me in a church that helps push me toward where You are calling me to be. I'm grateful for the foundation of holiness where my journey began as a young believer.

Lord, I surrender my plans, my ways, my desires, my body, and my heart to You. Forgive me for the times I've spoken negatively or doubted what You've called me to do. I pray that You continue to give me strength to face every battle that may come to test my faith. Teach me to stay rooted in Your Word and not become distracted by the patterns of this world.

Help me to lean on the promise of Isaiah 26:3, *"Thou wilt keep him in perfect peace, whose mind is stayed on thee: because he trusteth in thee."* I'm reminded that if I keep my mind on You, You will keep me in perfect peace.

Lord, teach me to trust the process You are taking me through, even when I don't understand it, even when it feels like an emotional roller coaster. Help me not to get caught up in my own plans that I lose sight of Your will for my life.

In Jesus' Name,
Amen.

Reflection Questions
1. Do I trust God enough to know He knows what's best?
2. Am I praying for God's will to be done in every area of my life?
3. Why am I fearful if I know His plans are going to give me a bright future?
4. Am I missing something by doing my own will?

UNLOCKING YOUR PURPOSE

Chapter Six:
Distractions That Kept Me from Pursuing My Purpose

If someone had told me years ago that there was purpose behind everything I would go through, I probably would've thought they were crazy. When I reflect on all I have experienced so far in my life from failing tests, falling in with the wrong crowd, being cursed out, having negative words spoken over me, teachers not taking me seriously, and being talked about for simply doing the right thing, it's a lot. It all made me want to completely shut down.

Even as a young believer, there were times I wanted to hide, afraid that people wouldn't take me seriously. But through those painful moments, I learned the value of prayer, fasting, consecrating myself, and staying grounded in God's Word. Having reliable, praying leaders I could lean on helped me, but I had to put in the work too.

When I failed major tests while in school that dictated if I would go to the next grade level, it was devastating. But prayer and reading Scripture helped me hold on. I began to find stories in the Bible that mirrored what I was facing, people who struggled with impossible situations but still overcame by faith. The Word reminded me who I was and what God said about me. I had to pray more, fast more, and decree God's promises over my life daily. I'd revisit my journal and reflect on sermons from my leaders that gave me strength.

There were many nights I cried myself to sleep, wondering if things would ever get better. But I kept pressing. I would fast before school, pray early in the morning, listen to worship music while getting ready, and pray throughout the day. That consistency helped me stay focused and avoid distractions.
Have you ever been so caught up in something that you forgot why you were doing it? That's what distractions do, they cloud our purpose. But the Word of God became my anchor. I began to speak over myself:

- I am courageous.
- I am smart.
- I am intelligent.

Psalm 139:14 says, *"I will praise thee; for I am fearfully and wonderfully made: marvelous are thy works; and that my soul knoweth right well."* And Jeremiah 31:3 reminds me that God loves me with an everlasting love.

One thing I've learned is this: when you're truly called by God, other people's opinions don't matter. You have to stay focused on the assignment He's given you. I spent years trapped in the mental box of others' negative words. But when I joined New Generation Church, everything shifted.

Even though I was living saved and seeking the Holy Ghost, I still struggled. The more I sought God, the more I realized that those painful experiences were preparing me for my purpose. I had to release years of baggage and recognize that I was becoming my own hindrance.

Hebrews 12:1–2 reminds us, *"Let us lay aside every weight, and the sin which doth so easily beset us... Looking unto Jesus the author and finisher of our faith..."* If Jesus endured the cross for us, surely we can push through trials and distractions for Him.

Sometimes, we are the very ones keeping ourselves from purpose because we won't release what God is asking us to let go. Ask yourself:

- What is God asking me to release so I can live?
- What steps can I take to stay focused on His plan for my life?
- We have a choice: heal and grow or hold onto pain.

Deuteronomy 30:19 says, *"I have set before you life and death, blessing and cursing: therefore choose life...* " God wants us to choose life, but that means letting go of distractions.

I struggled deeply when I failed the STAAR tests. I felt like a failure and questioned everything. *Why did this happen to me? Am I not smart enough? Why did I have to endure this?* I didn't understand. I became depressed. It became hard to pray or even trust God.

But I thank God for praying leaders who never gave up on me. Their intercession reminded me that God won't let you quit, even when you feel like it. When God says "No," or when prayers go unanswered, we have to examine our motives.

James 4:3 says, *"Ye ask, and receive not, because ye ask amiss... "* This taught me to align my desires with God's will, not my own.

So again I ask you: What has you so distracted that you can't focus on God?

In Luke 10:38–42, Martha was distracted by serving while Mary sat at Jesus' feet. Jesus said Mary chose the better part. This story reminds us not to be so busy doing for God that we miss time with God.

When I transitioned to college, distractions only increased. I knew the God I served, yet temptations came, people, parties, and opportunities that could've led me away from Him. I was excited for a new season,

but I also remembered what had been instilled in me: holiness, standards, and a desire to please God.
Every semester brought choices, compromise or stay faithful. Matthew 6:24 says, *"No one can serve two masters..."* We can't serve both God and the world. It's hard sometimes. It gets lonely. But I've learned: you're never truly alone when you walk with God.

God will send the right people. He'll give you peace about where to go and who to connect with. He'll protect you from things you don't even realize you need protection from. Sometimes you just have to say, "That's not what I do." Be the example. Be the light that draws others back to Christ.

UNLOCKING YOUR PURPOSE

Dear God,

Thank You for the opportunity to grow through the storms, lessons, and trials that come my way. It's not always easy, but I know you've given me the strength and confidence to endure as a believer.

Lord, guide us through Your Word, which brings instruction, correction, encouragement, and wisdom. Help us stay focused on what you've called us to be. May we remain committed to prayer, fasting, and consecrating so we can receive clearer direction from you?

Teach us to trust your timing, your will, and your process, not our own. We release everything that tries to hinder us from pursuing our purpose, from seeking you in prayer, and from diving into Your Word. Remind us that what you have for us is far greater than anything we could imagine.

Help us to press through the hurt, the pain, the lies, the betrayal, and every distraction sent to break us. Let our faith be stronger than our fear, and our obedience louder than the noise around us.

In Jesus' Name,
Amen.

Reflection Questions
1. What is holding us back from going after everything God has for us?
2. Why is it so hard for me to release it?
3. What are some distractions I need to get rid of?
4. Why am I fighting the will of God?

UNLOCKING YOUR PURPOSE

Chapter Seven
Seeking the Lord About My Purpose

Have you ever doubted something simply because you were unsure of the path it would take you? That was me. Deep down, I knew I had purpose, but because I was consumed by struggles, it was hard for me to seek the Lord concerning it. I wrestled with so many things, doubt, insecurity, low self-esteem, and feelings of unworthiness. I had been in church all my life, but I never truly believed I had a divine assignment.

For the longest time, I couldn't imagine God using someone like me, especially so young. Thoughts constantly filled my mind: *I'm not qualified. I'm not equipped for this. I don't know what I'm doing. I don't meet the expectations.* James 1:6 says, *"But let him ask in faith, nothing wavering. For he that wavereth is like a wave of the sea driven with the wind and tossed."* That verse reminds us to believe God will fulfill His purpose in our lives, even when we can't yet see it. If we constantly entertain doubt, it becomes impossible to fully understand His purpose or guidance.

At the time, I couldn't see it clearly. I was still asking, *How am I supposed to live for God at such a young age?* I knew it would come with challenges. When I joined New Generation Church and truly gave my life to Christ, I began to develop a deeper relationship with Him. Still, I struggled with understanding my purpose, even after receiving prophetic words. In my mind, I wondered, *how am I going to walk this out when I still don't fully understand what God is calling me to do?*

Even so, I believed those prophecies would come to pass—in God's timing.

I remember receiving a word that I would preach the gospel. I had no idea that the Lord would begin using me in 2020, right in the middle of the pandemic, to launch my YouTube channel, ***JourneywithK.*** It wasn't something I had planned, and honestly, I had no desire to do it at first. But when the Lord told me to start, I wanted to be sure it was from Him and not just a random thought. God confirmed it again in my spirit.

That was the beginning of God calling me to be a vessel, encouraging others through His Word.

One of the things God placed deeply in my spirit was this: *Encourage the people. Don't let them give up. Tell them to stay focused, stay alert, stay watchful.* Colossians 3:2 says, *"Set your affection on things above, not on things on the earth."* That Scripture helps keep me spiritually grounded. It reminds me not to get caught up in the natural distractions; likes, shares, or followers.

God moved through every single video I posted. The comments I received were powerful and often brought me to tears—proof that the obedience was worth it. It's not about the numbers for me. It's about drawing people from all walks of life to Christ. I pray over every video I post because I want the Holy Spirit to lead me in everything I do. When we seek God concerning our purpose, even the smallest idea can be the beginning of something greater.

The more time I spent with God, the more He revealed—about who He is, what He expects, and even the difference between praise and worship. Every spiritual encounter gave me more insight into my purpose. Looking back, I see that even in middle school and high school, the storms I endured were purposeful.

When I first joined the ministry, I began writing encouraging letters to my leaders. I had doubts, *would this even matter to them?* But I followed God's leading anyway. I just wanted to encourage them, so that if they ever had a rough day, they could look back on those words and feel seen, strengthened, and uplifted.

What I didn't realize then was that through every letter, God was showing me my purpose, piece by piece.

Writing wasn't just something I liked, it was something I was anointed to do. God was using my hands to release healing, hope, and strength.

Throughout college, especially in my freshman and sophomore years, I made intentional time to fast, pray, and seek God's face. I wanted to be sure I was hearing Him clearly. I ask you to reflect for a moment: *Am I really seeking the face of God? Or am I rushing into something because it feels right in the moment?*

Deuteronomy 5:33 reminds us, *"Ye shall walk in all the ways which the LORD your God hath commanded you, that ye may live... and that it may be well with you."* Obedience keeps us on His path—and His path is the one that leads to true life.

As I continued writing those letters, God started showing me that my calling was bigger than just encouraging leaders in my church. In my junior year of college, I had a writing assignment for one of my classes. While completing it, I had an undeniable encounter with God. He reminded me: *It's not just about the words you write, it's about the anointing I've placed on you. You carry the power to push people into their next.* That was my confirmation. God had anointed me to write—not just in letters or classroom assignments, but to impact the world.

If you're reading this, I encourage you to seek God about your own purpose. Ask Him for *real* confirmation, not just a revelation that comes from emotion or excitement. Sometimes, the answers you're looking for won't come overnight. This will be a process. A journey. And when you're truly seeking Him, sometimes it means silencing the outside noise, taking a break from social media, turning off notifications, and spending quiet, uninterrupted time in His presence.

The confirmations I received didn't come instantly. They came through prayer, fasting, and obedience. Mark 9:29 says, *"This kind can come forth by nothing, but by prayer and fasting."* We have to be willing to press in. I knew God was confirming my writing assignment when my leaders began telling me how much they needed those letters. Hearing that brought me to tears. It was no one but God leading me through it all.

Sometimes, your confirmation will come through people. Other times, through impact. I began receiving messages from people on YouTube who were being encouraged and strengthened by the motivational videos, and I knew it wasn't about me. It was about what God wanted to do through me.

UNLOCKING YOUR PURPOSE

Ask yourself: *Am I doing this to please people, or to please God?*

Whatever God has called you to do, stay focused. Stay watchful. I know it can be scary and uncomfortable, but walk in boldness. I was once fearful to even write letters. I questioned if anyone would even read them. I worried that people would scroll past my videos. But I prayed, *Lord, give me the courage to keep going.*

If I had let fear win, I wouldn't be doing what I'm doing today.

Have you ever allowed fear to stop you from walking in purpose? Maybe it's writing a book, launching a podcast, starting a business, or going back to school. 2 Timothy 1:7 says, *"For God hath not given us the spirit of fear, but of power, and of love, and of a sound mind."*

I pray this chapter challenges you to walk in boldness, and to seek the face of God as you walk in everything He's calling you to do.

Dear God,

Today, I thank You because You are with us every step of the way on our journey. I thank You that when we seek You, You hear our cries, our petitions, and the desires of our hearts. Your Word says in Psalm 34:17, *"The righteous cry, and the Lord heareth, and delivereth them out of all their troubles."*

Lord, forgive us for being consumed by our problems, struggles, and storms, for those moments when we forget that You are in full control of every situation. I pray that You help us to release it all into Your hands, knowing that You care deeply for us.

Teach us to seek You like never before so that we may clearly understand what You've called us to do in this world. Help us to apply the Word of God to our lives, even in those low moments when we struggle to see a way out.

Lord, order our steps as we continue to pursue a deeper understanding of who You are. Help us to stand firm on what You have already spoken over our lives. We declare that fear, doubt, insecurity, and low self-esteem will no longer have a hold over our future.

We speak life, we speak victory, prosperity, and good success over everything we touch and put our minds to. Let it flourish for Your glory. And Lord, grant us patience as we walk through this journey called purpose.

In Jesus' Name,
Amen.

Reflection Questions

1. Am I making movements for the applause of people?
2. Am I allowing God to order my steps?
3. What is stopping me from achieving my goals?
4. Did I pray before rushing into this?

UNLOCKING YOUR PURPOSE

Chapter Eight:
Strategies that helped me to unlock my purpose

I believe it's important for us to understand what purpose is, how we identify it, and the impact our purpose can have on many lives. As a young believer, I've learned through my Christian walk that we will endure trials, but we serve a God who comes through every time. In the midst of all we face, storms, struggles, victories, and losses, there is purpose. God uses every part of our journey for His glory.

I've never been more dedicated to God and my relationship with Him than I am now. I've come to understand that He allows us to go through things to test our faith and prepare us for what's ahead. My journey as a young Christian has been key to unlocking my purpose. It's shown me that purpose is much bigger than me. The encounters I've had with God have led me to seek Him more deeply, bringing fresh revelations about my purpose. My relationship with God has given me a new perspective, even on the trials I've had to face. It has helped me distinguish between decisions made from fleshly assumptions and those led by His Spirit.

Understanding Purpose

When it comes to purpose, I want us to reflect not on what we gain, but on how we can impact others. Some of us may already know our purpose, while others may still be searching. Either way, our mindset should shift from obligation to obedience from "I have to" to "God, use me however You will."

I will forever be grateful for the leadership I sit under. When I think about where I started, lost in life and in Christ, they helped push me into a new dimension in God. Ephesians 2:10 reminds us, *"For we are His workmanship, created in Christ Jesus unto good works, which God hath before ordained that we should walk in them."* That verse is proof that we are vessels created to bring Him glory.

Growing up, I knew I wanted to help people. I didn't know if that meant being a doctor, teacher, fashion designer, or counselor. But over time, especially through writing in journals, school papers, and letters, I realized God was calling me to write. What He places on our hearts to say—especially on paper, is often where purpose begins to unfold.

The Role of Prayer

Prayer is essential when seeking to unlock your purpose. For me, developing a prayer life that includes fasting, reading the Word, and consecration has been a major key.

As a young believer, fasting for me looked like turning off my phone, putting it on "Do Not Disturb," and sacrificing food and drink for four hours. I'd fill that time with prayer, meditating on scripture, and worship music. It wasn't always easy, but I learned that when we make the sacrifice, God meets us there.

Psalm 34:15 says, "The eyes of the Lord are upon the righteous, and His ears are open unto their cry." That reminds me our efforts aren't in vain, God hears us. Unlocking our purpose often comes through seasons of prayer, where we hear clear instructions from Him.

I remember seeking God for direction about my purpose from the time I was at my granny's church, and later at New Generation Church. That's where God began to reveal it, piece by piece, especially during my college journey.

There were moments I'd question myself: *Lord, are You sure? What if I mess up? What if no one reads what I write?* But even after being saved and filled with the Holy Ghost, I kept asking God to show me. My prayer was, *Lord, help me make a difference in whatever You've assigned me to do. Let others see You—not me—in my writing and my speaking.*

Practical Steps to Unlock Your Purpose

While spiritual tools like prayer and fasting are vital, I also had to use natural tools. I started by researching my interests. What did I enjoy doing that didn't feel like an obligation? What were my passions?

In middle school, I took a career assessment test to identify my strengths, interests, and potential career paths. I enjoyed English, though I didn't know then that writing would be the route God would guide me to. Looking back, I see how all the research, school projects, and counselor advice played a role in helping me discover that passion.

Remember: this is a *process.* You won't always get the answer in a single day. Philippians 1:6 encourages us: "Being confident of this very thing, that He which hath begun a good work in you will perform it until the day of Jesus Christ." Let that be your reminder, God finishes what He starts.

UNLOCKING YOUR PURPOSE

If you're unsure about your purpose right now, ask yourself:

- What do I enjoy doing in my free time?
- Is it cooking, sewing, reading, writing, and teaching?
- Can I see myself doing this long-term?

Keep praying as you are researching your passion. Don't rush the process or give in to societal pressure. Take your time. Bathe your search in prayer. Remember, God's timing is perfect.

UNLOCKING YOUR PURPOSE

Dear God,

I thank You for the strategies You have given us to accomplish everything You are calling us to do. Lord, forgive us for the times we have been doubtful, fearful, or spoken negativity over our future. I pray that You connect us with the right people and resources that will push us further into our purpose. Help us to trust the process, Your plan, and Your will for our lives.

Lord, may we understand that this is a journey and that You will grant us the patience and endurance to persevere, especially when we don't receive immediate answers. Cover our hearts, minds, and spirits from discouragement, fear, and doubt. Help us to remember that everything we face in this world, and everything we are believing You for, will unfold in Your perfect timing.

I pray that every gift, dream, goal, and passion we have will be unlocked for Your glory. May we put on our spiritual glasses to recognize that everything we do, say, and have can be used for Your purpose. I pray that the tools shared in this book will bless and guide everyone who encounters them.

In Jesus' Name,
Amen.

Reflection Questions

1. What are your passions, and how do they align with God's purpose for your life?
2. How can you incorporate prayer and fasting into your daily routine to seek His guidance?
3. Are there any fears or doubts holding you back? How can you surrender them to God?

Chapter Nine:
What It Means to Unlock Your Purpose

When it comes to unlocking your purpose, everyone's path will look different. Some may take longer than others, but it's a process, don't rush it. Unlocking your purpose simply means discovering what you've been called to do and how it will impact the world, bringing glory to our Heavenly Father. Since I've unlocked my purpose, it hasn't always been easy, but I know it's worth it because God has greater things in store for us all.

There are still moments when I step into my purpose fully, but I am choosing to trust God every step of the way. I still have my "what if" moments, questioning myself because I'm young, but I've learned to push through and let God anoint me even more as I continue to be an example. I remember many times when I was called to serve in church, but fear held me back. I worried about how things would turn out, would I get embarrassed? Would they take me seriously? What if someone criticized me? I had all these "what ifs" swirling in my mind, but I had to shift my focus from those fears to the assignment God had given me. I had to stop worrying about what others might say, think, or the insecurities the enemy tried to plant in my head.

UNLOCKING YOUR PURPOSE

There were times I doubted myself so much, questioning whether I was qualified, whether they were sure they wanted me to do this, or if anyone would see the God in me. I had to ask God to shift my focus when I was called to do something because I realized I was giving it too much of my attention. It was about God and what He might be trying to do in those moments, not about me.

If someone were to ask me what unlocking your purpose looks like, I would say it means stepping out of your comfort zone to do what God has called you to do, no matter what people might say, how they might look at you, or the insecurities and doubts that try to hinder you. Stay focused on the assignment, not on worldly distractions or negative thoughts. One of the biggest struggles I've had as a young believer is learning to tune out negative comments, people, and the "what ifs," but I've learned to focus on the objective instead of worrying about how people perceive me.

One tool I use when dealing with fear and negativity is speaking the Word of God over my life daily, like affirmations. The Word of God is so powerful that when you speak it, it has to be manifested in your life. My prayer has been, "Lord, teach me to utilize the power You've given me through Your Word." So, if you have to step out, even if you're scared, anxious, or unsure, just do it.

Being a young believer for God won't be easy, and you'll face moments that make you question whether pursuing your purpose is worth it. There have been plenty of times when I felt alone, even after being saved, filled with the Holy Ghost, and still striving to find my purpose. I had to learn to seek God's face through everything. There will be seasons where you'll have to go through things by yourself and rely solely on God. Psalm 55:22 says, *"Cast thy burden upon the LORD, and he shall sustain thee: he shall never suffer the righteous to be moved."* When you give your burdens to the Lord, He will guide you through whatever you're facing, even when things don't seem well.

I believe it's crucial to be ready and willing to do what God calls you to do in order to unlock your purpose. I can testify to this because I'm in a season where I'm choosing to be a yielded vessel for God, whatever He may call me to do. Every time I'm asked to speak, pray, or exhort, I feel nervous. The enemy tries to bring anxiety and doubts to my mind, and I sometimes wonder if I should ask the person if they're sure they want me to do this. But I consistently remind myself of what God's Word says. Sometimes it looks scary, and we don't know what's ahead, but knowing He's with us every step of the way is enough to keep us going.

UNLOCKING YOUR PURPOSE

As we unlock our purpose and walk in God's calling, it's vital to stay focused on the task at hand because, if not, it can consume us. Stepping out in faith to do the work of Christ may be uncomfortable at times, but remember that God is with you wherever you go. Representing Christ, especially as a young person, can be intimidating and overwhelming. You never know how people will respond when you're called to certain places, speaking to others, or simply trying to encourage someone. But often, you just have to take that step of faith.

John 15:16 reminds us: *"Ye have not chosen me, but I have chosen you, and ordained you, that ye should go and bring forth fruit, and that your fruit should remain: that whatsoever ye shall ask of the Father in my name, he may give it you.* "You didn't choose God, He chose you for such a time as this. Remember, you've been equipped to do the work of the Lord.

When it comes to unlocking my purpose, it means being completely submitted to whatever God calls me to do, no matter what may come or who may leave. We must learn to trust God, even through the unknown and whatever mountains or valleys we encounter. Keep trusting Him because God will never lead you on a path He's not on. Our prayer should be: *"Lord, help us to be ready for what You're calling us to, and help us walk through the purpose You've given us according to Your will."*

As we close this chapter, I pray you are encouraged and motivated to unlock your purpose. There will be times when you may not receive the answers you're looking for right away, but when you continue to seek God's face, He will begin to reveal it to you piece by piece, like a puzzle. I'm reminded that it's crucial to stay on track and not try to force our own puzzle piece into God's plan.

Matthew 6:33 says, *"But seek ye first the kingdom of God, and his righteousness; and all these things shall be added unto you."* We must be willing to seek Him until our focus shifts.

I challenge you to take a moment and ask yourself: *What blocks are hindering me from unlocking my purpose? What can I do to fully unlock what God is trying to reveal to me?*

Dear God,

I thank You for helping me recognize how to unlock my purpose, for showing me what it looks like, and for providing the tools to get there. Lord, forgive me if I have been my own hindrance in unlocking my purpose in You.

I pray that You would help me trust You fully as I step into my purpose. Lord, I ask for Your will to be done in every area of my life so that I can fulfill what You've called me to do. Help me, Lord, to not only read Your Word, but to apply it to my own life, allowing it to guide my every step.

We trust You in the development stage, and now we believe You to guide us through this unlocking stage. I decree and declare that we will not quit, give in, or give up, even when the answers we've been praying for have not yet come.

Lord, take control of our thoughts, emotions, and journey as we walk through this day by day.

In Jesus' Name,
Amen.

Reflection Questions

1. Did God release me to step out or is this my flesh?
2. Did I ask God for guidance concerning this?
3. Am I trying to force this?
4. Are you willing to submit fully to God?

UNLOCKING YOUR PURPOSE

Chapter Ten
What My Walk Looks Like Now

"Encounters with God"

My journey as a young believer in Christ has been nothing short of amazing. I am more committed and dedicated to God than ever before. Through reading the Word of God, praying, fasting, consecrating, praising, worshiping, and so much more, I've learned countless lessons. Even in the midst of storms, struggles, and times when my faith was tested, I had encounters with God that transformed my life.

I remember when I lost loved ones who were so dear to me, and I felt like I couldn't pray anymore. I got on my knees in my dorm room, and as I began praying for something else, the Holy Spirit interceded on my behalf. By the time I finished praying, I felt so much better than when I first started. Romans 8:26 reminds us: *"Likewise the Spirit also helpeth our infirmities: for we know not what we should pray for as we ought: but the Spirit itself maketh intercession for us with groanings which cannot be uttered."* It's so important to have the Holy Spirit, because when we don't know what to pray, He intercedes for us. In that moment, I realized that God uses our lowest points to bring something greater out of us. Those low places teaches us not to complain, but instead will often give us a new perspective. To experience the presence of God is a privilege and an honor—not everyone gets to encounter that.

"Remaining Faithful"

Since I've been at New Generation Church, my journey as a believer has transformed in countless ways. I've learned so much, from the power of a simple prayer to the depth of God's Word. I've experienced His presence like never before and discovered the difference between praising God and worshiping Him. In those moments of worship, I've encountered God in ways that have humbled me and shifted my heart to a place I never thought could be possible.

When I first came to Christ, I felt that no one would be there to help me seek the Holy Spirit or guide me in staying saved. But when I was filled with the Holy Spirit, I had people around me who helped and supported me, there was no feeling of being alone. This experience, being saved and filled with the Holy Spirit, shaped me in a way that has carried me through every season of my life. When I went to college, I knew how to respond in prayer when situations arose. I knew how to connect with like-minded believers and avoid paths that could have led me away from God.

John 14:26 says, *"But the Comforter, which is the Holy Ghost, whom the Father will send in my name, he shall teach you all things, and bring all things to your remembrance, whatsoever I have said unto you."* I love this scripture because it's helped me through so many challenging times. One of the things I love about God is that He is with you every step of the way as you become a new creation in Him. However, He doesn't force you to submit; He welcomes you with open arms.

"Learning Who I Am in Christ"

Another significant thing I've learned on my journey with Christ is who I am in Him and the spiritual inheritance I've been given. For so long, I didn't know who I was or what my future held because I was consumed by what others said and the hardships I had to endure, bad company, harsh words, and negativity. I remember going to church, saved and seeking God, reading His Word, praying, fasting, and consecrating, but still struggling with my identity in Christ.

There were times I had to keep seeking the Lord through prayer and His Word to help me understand who I am in Him. Sometimes, life's challenges can cloud the way God sees us. It's vital to stay focused and speak God's Word over your life, both when things are good and when things are not. The more I sought God, the more He revealed to me who I truly am.
It's through the storms that God begins to show us things, developing us and shifting our perspectives. I've learned not to be ashamed of the gospel or who God created me to be. In high school, I struggled with

making friends while also trying to live according to God's purpose for my life. I learned that you can't please everyone, so I chose to live for Christ and not be ashamed. I knew that if I prayed for the right friends, God would send them.

Living for God as a young person comes with challenges, and I've faced many. But as I've grown in Christ, being saved, and filled with the Holy Spirit, I've remained prayerful. I realize that many young people struggle with fear and insecurity, wondering what might happen if they truly surrender things to God. I began writing because I believe God is calling me to be a leader, a young woman who lives for Him, serves with humility, and represents holiness without compromising my standards.

As a young believer, dealing with insecurity and fear of what others might think was a constant struggle that tested my faith. One thing I would tell anyone is to remain true to who God made you to be. Don't let anyone change you. Psalm 139:16 says, *"Thine eyes did see my substance, yet being unperfect; and in thy book all my members were written, which in continuance were fashioned, when as yet there was none of them."* God knows everything about us before we were even born, and His desire is for us to embrace our unique selves, not conform to what the world expects.

I had to learn to be myself, even if that meant keeping some relationships at a distance. When I dealt with insecurity, I had to use God's Word as daily affirmations to remind myself of who I am in Christ. As I consistently spoke His Word over my life, those insecurities slowly faded. Take a moment to reflect: how many times have you allowed insecurities to stop you from doing what you're called to do? I challenge you to speak God's Word over your life every day until it becomes a part of your spirit and mind.

For so long, I gave the enemy too much power in my thoughts, especially around insecurities and fear of what others might say. I allowed people and the enemy to keep me in a box, afraid to speak or act. But with prayer and time spent in God's presence, I broke free from that fear. It wasn't until I came to New Generation Church that I truly began walking in freedom, no longer feeling like I was confined.

To anyone reading this, I want to encourage you to keep going. Keep persevering, no matter where you are in your walk with God. Don't let anyone or anything stop you from pursuing what God has called you to do.

Reflection Questions:
1. How many times have you allowed the enemy to make you run from your purpose?
2. Why do we allow fear to stop us?
3. Imagine what happens when you start speaking the Word of God over your life?
4. Am I spending enough time with God?

Dear God,

Today, I thank You for every lesson, teaching, storm, struggle, low place, and high place You have allowed me to experience. I now recognize that all of it is part of Your divine plan, leading me to where You are guiding me. Lord, I pray that whoever reads this will be empowered, equipped, and encouraged to keep fighting and pressing forward to accomplish what You have called us to do.

Teach us, Lord, to rely on Your Word, for it is in Your Word that we find our hope, strength, guidance, and wisdom. We ask for Your continued outpouring on our lives, so we may persevere on this journey You've set before us. Help us, Lord, to not grow weary or overwhelmed in the days to come. May we trust in the path You've placed us on.

In Jesus' Name,
Amen.

About the Author

Kellie Williams is a native of Desoto, Texas. As a daughter, sister, cousin and friend, she values her family and holds close meaningful relationships. In December 2018, she received her Bachelor of Arts degree in English with a minor in Communication Studies at Texas A&M University Commerce. During her academic years, she discovered her passion for writing was bigger than her and gained motivation by her desire to push others just as others had pushed her. As a young and sanctified woman of God, she has embraced her calling to live for Christ while encouraging others on their journey to purpose. In September 7, 2020, she created an online YouTube platform, entitled "Journey with K", where she provides encouragement and motivation for people who desire to draw closer to God. She is a proud member of New Generation Church where she serves as the local Youth Chairlady and part of the Women's Department Leadership team. Kellie Williams has a deep passion for the things of God and is committed to being a vessel for Jesus Christ.

Connect with me:

Instagram:_imblessed_22

Facebook: Kellie Williams

YouTube: JourneywithK22

www.ingramcontent.com/pod-product-compliance
Lightning Source LLC
Chambersburg PA
CBHW071330130626
46556CB00004B/1834